That's Just What I Needed Today

Quotes from the world's most inspirational thinkers

NAN RAE

DEDICATION

To all the voices of hope in our world.

Cover art: Nan Rae: Japan's First Love
Text set in Calligraphic 421, Zapfino and Minion Pro

Copyright © 2020 Nan Rae
NANRAESTUDIO.COM

A joint production of Nan Rae Studio and Laughing Elephant Books

First published in 2020 by
LAUGHING ELEPHANT BOOKS
PO Box 632871
San Diego, CA 92163

LAUGHINGELEPHANTBOOKS.com

First printing 2020

Printed in China

ACKNOWLEDGEMENTS

No sooner had the ink dried on "WHAT IF...", than my intrepid publisher, Benjamin Darling at Laughing Elephant Books, asked for my next book so yet again he is responsible for the following pages.

Most importantly, my thanks for "THAT'S JUST WHAT I NEEDED TODAY" have to go to all my extraordinary followers on Instagram and Facebook who, when seeing postings on Nan Rae Fine Art, respond so beautifully to not only the art but as much to the inspirational quotes posted along with the artwork with so many writing, "This was just what I needed today". It became clear what this book would be.

These quotes inspired me and so there would be no book without them. For all the authors I send my love from a most grateful heart.

My thanks again to Veronica Carrasco who brings everything to fruition and is as my student, Brian Foster so aptly said Veronica is my secret weapon. Special thanks to Lucia Moskal, my brilliant, literate friend who was beyond generous in editing my acknowledgments and introduction. And, I'd be remiss if I failed to mention Judith Rochelle Nelson who continually overwhelmed me as she spread the joy of "WHAT IF…" to everyone in her vast universe, encouraging me to create this next book.

INTRODUCTION

I wrote "WHAT IF...We Have the Power to Change Our Lives" to express what I have learned throughout my journey… which is to be open, relaxing into my life, letting go of fear and above all….being joyful. Of course gratitude and a sense that I am loved beyond comprehension by my creator tops the list and has always pointed the way for me. So that book was a bit of a 'how to' or really ways I've found to let go and fully embrace my life and find my purpose.

For "THAT'S JUST WHAT I NEEDED TODAY… Quotes From the World's Most Inspirational Thinkers," it became clear to me that we all need inspirational sayings from people we admire. People who have struggled with their humanity and won the battle over ego, selfishness and most importantly conquered fear. The best place to start was with the quotes that received the most likes as they were posted alongside my artwork on the Nan Rae Fine Art Instagram and Facebook pages. In fact, the title is in itself a direct quote from many of my followers as they wrote, "That's just what I needed today!" Compiling these inspirational quotes into book form has been a source of great joy as I connected with my amazing followers by reading their comments yet again and putting into book form what they have loved the most.

My hope is that these pages speak to your heart and contain a blessing as you embark on each day's journey. I send you love.

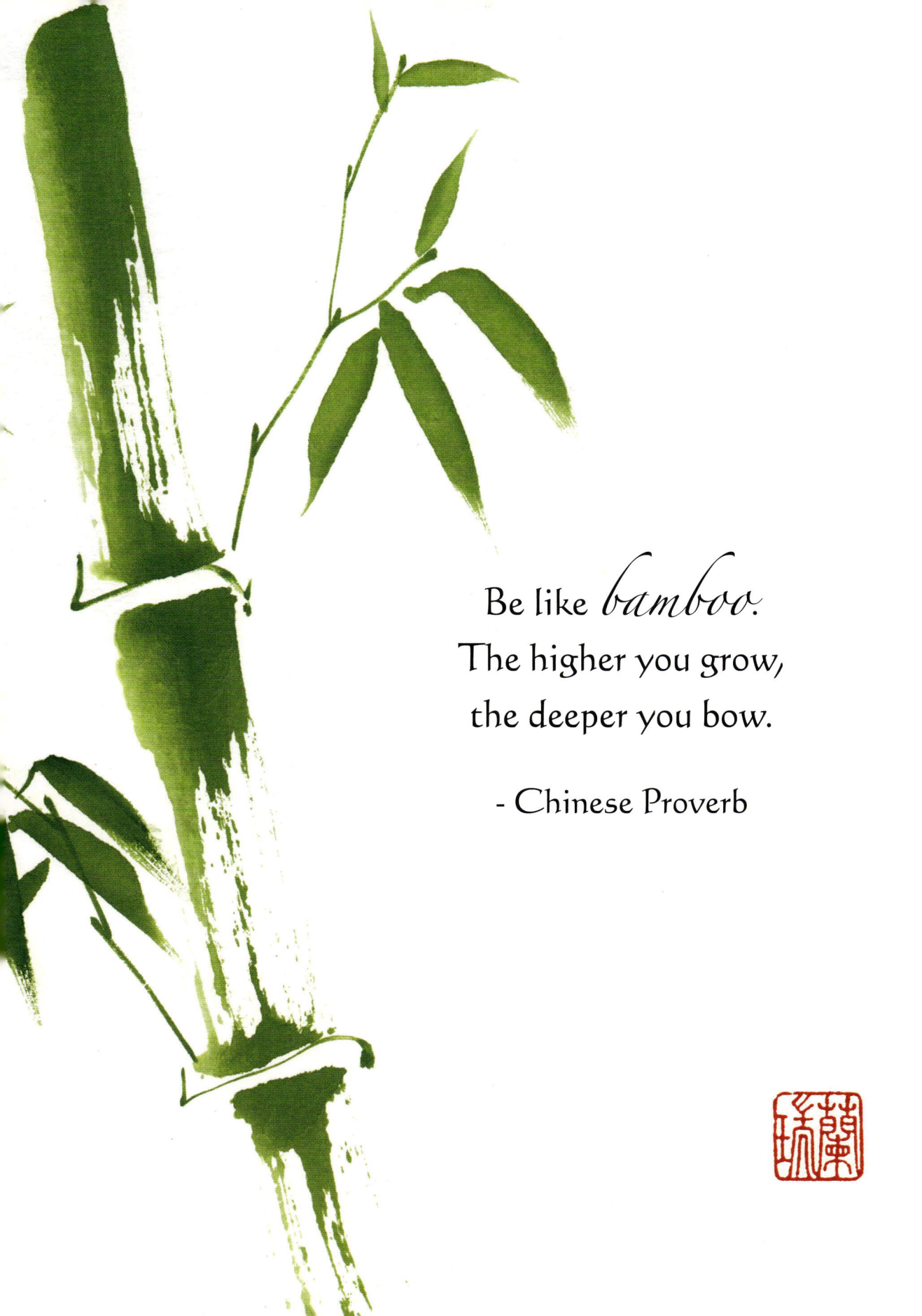

Be like *bamboo.*
The higher you grow,
the deeper you bow.

- Chinese Proverb

Remember, the thing you strive for isn't perfection;
it's not the easy win or the avoidance of failure.

It's the *gift of growth,*

the *opportunity for evolution.*

Life in a box is not life well lived.

- Jonathan Fields

Peace is present right here and now,
in ourselves and in everything we do and see.
Every breath we take, every step we take,
can be filled with *peace, joy, and serenity.*

The question is whether or not
we are in touch with it.
We need only to be *awake,*
alive in the present moment.

- Thich Nhat Hanh

It is good to *love*
many things,
for therein lies the
true strength,
and whosoever loves
much performs much,
and can
accomplish much,
and what is done in
love is well done.

- Vincent Van Gogh

Your *destiny* is to fulfill those things upon which you focus most intently.

So choose to *keep your focus* on that which is truly *magnificent, beautiful, uplifting and joyful.*

Your life is always moving toward something.

- Ralph Marston

Living in the moment

means letting go of the past
and not waiting for the future.

It means

living your life consciously,

aware that

each moment you breathe is a gift.

- Oprah Winfrey

The *artist* is the confidant of nature,
flowers carry on dialogues with him through
the graceful bending of their stems
and the harmoniously tinted nuances
of their blossoms.

Every *flower* has a cordial word

which nature directs towards him.

- Auguste Rodin

What sets you apart

can sometimes feel
like a burden and it's not.
And a lot of the time,

it's what makes you great.

- Emma Stone

While it may seem small,
the ripple effects of

small things
is

extraordinary.

- Matt Bevin

The whole point of being alive
is to *evolve* into the complete person
you were intended to be.

- Oprah Winfrey

There is a vitality, a life force,
a quickening that is translated through *you* into action,

and there is only one of you in all time,
this expression is unique,
and if you block it,
it will never exist through any other medium;
and be lost.
The world will not have it.
It is not your business to determine how good it is,
not how it compares with other expression.
It is your business to keep it yours clearly and directly,
to keep the channel open.
You do not even have to believe in yourself or your work.
You have to keep open and aware directly to the urges
that motivate you.

Keep the channel open.

No artist is pleased.
There is no satisfaction whatever at any time.
There is only a queer, divine dissatisfaction,
a blessed unrest that keeps us marching and makes us
more alive than the others.

- Martha Graham

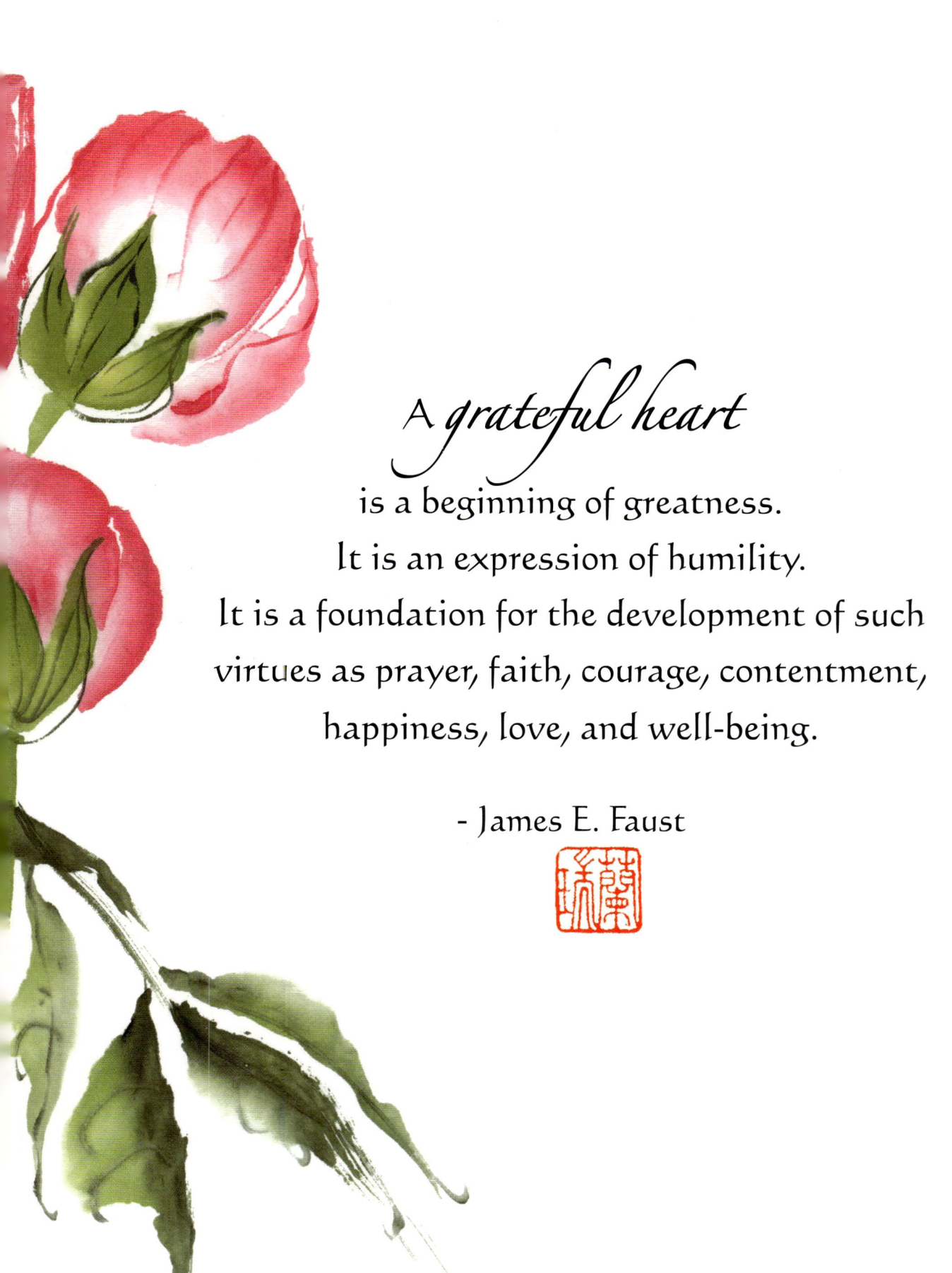

A *grateful heart*

is a beginning of greatness.
It is an expression of humility.
It is a foundation for the development of such
virtues as prayer, faith, courage, contentment,
happiness, love, and well-being.

- James E. Faust

A *beautiful life* is not a place
at which you arrive,
but the experience you *create*
moment by moment.

- Lebo Grand

Explore,

Experience,

Then *Push Beyond.*

- Aaron Lauritsen

Reach out and *help* others.

If you have the power

to make someone *happy*, do it.

Be a *vessel,* be the *change,* be the *difference,*

or be the *inspiration*.

Shine your light

as an example.

The world needs more of that.
- Germany Kent

As we begin to
love and appreciate ourselves
as we are,

our channels open and

we access the

infinite vitality of life force.

- Shakti Gawain

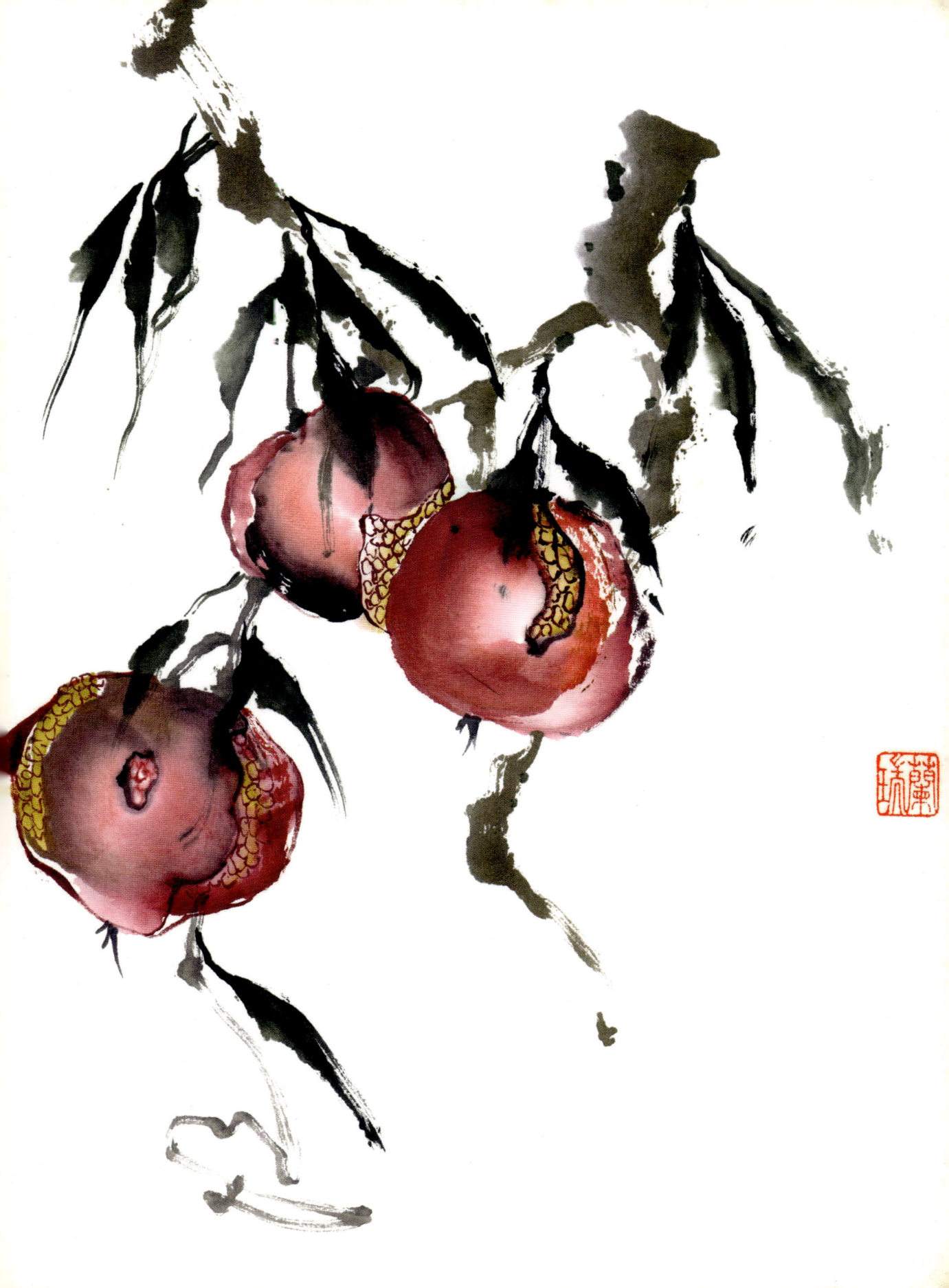

What *sunshine* is to *flowers*,
smiles are to *humanity*.
These are but trifles,
to be sure;
but scattered along life's pathway,
the good they do is inconceivable.

- Joseph Addison

The more *generous* we are,

the more *joyous* we become.

The more *cooperative* we are,

the more *valuable* we become.

The more *enthusiastic* we are,

the more *productive* we become.

The more *serving* we are,

the more *prosperous* we become.

- William Arthur Ward

Become totally *empty*

Quiet the restlessness of the mind
Only then will you witness everything
unfolding from emptiness.

See all things flourish and dance
in endless variation

And once again merge back
into perfect emptiness

—

Their true repose
Their true nature
Emerging, flourishing,
dissolving back again
This is the eternal process of return
To know this process brings
enlightenment.

- Lao Tzu

The most incredible *beauty*

and the most satisfying way of life come
from affirming
your own uniqueness.

- Jane Fonda

Each day brings new
opportunities,
allowing you to constantly
live with *love*—
be there for others —
bring a little *light*
into someone's day.

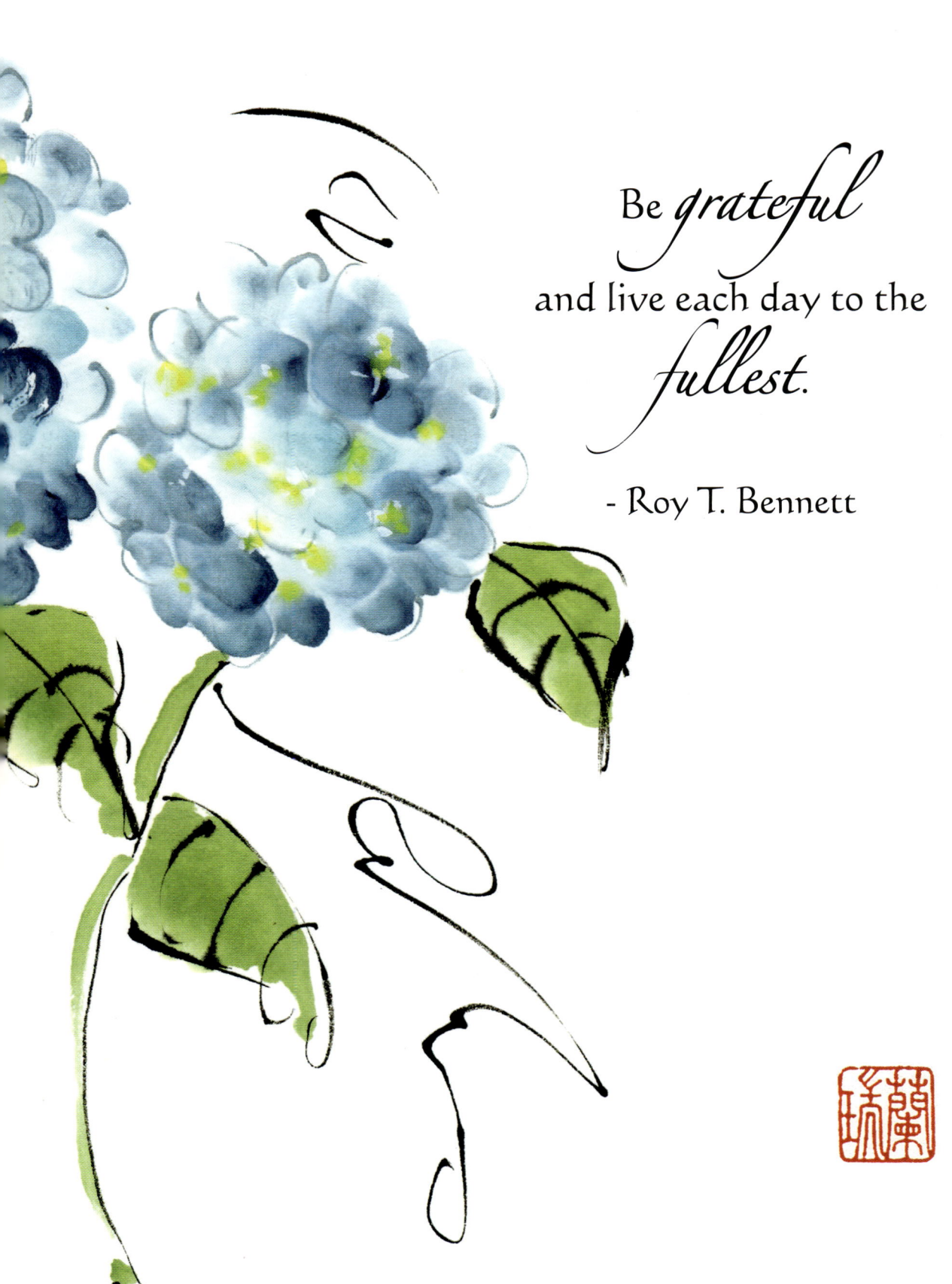

Be *grateful*
and live each day to the
fullest.

- Roy T. Bennett

The only person you are destined to become
is the
person you decide to be.

- Ralph Waldo Emerson

This *life* is *yours*.

Take the *power to choose*
what you want to do and do it well.

Take the *power to love*

what you want in life and love it honestly.

Take the power to walk in the forest
and be a part of nature.

Take the *power to control*

your own life.

No one else can do it for you.

Take the *power to make*

your life *happy*.

- Susan Polis Schutz

Free yourself

from the burden of feeling the need to
hold on to anything.
Let go...
you are a part of everything.

- Steve Maraboli

Love life.
Engage in it.
Give it all you've got.
Love it with a passion
because
life truly does give back,
many times over, what you put into it.

- Maya Angelou

Dare to Be

When a new day begins,
dare to *smile* gratefully.

When there is darkness,
dare to be the first to *shine a light*

When there is injustice,
dare to be the first to *condemn it*.

When something seems difficult,
dare to *do it anyway*.

When life seems to beat you down,
dare to *fight back*.

When there seems to be no hope,
dare to *find* some.

When you're feeling tired,

dare to *keep going.*

When times are tough,

dare to *be tougher.*

When love hurts you,

dare to *love again.*

When someone is hurting,

dare to *help them heal.*

When another is lost,

dare to help them *find the way.*

When a friend falls,

dare to be the first to *extend a hand.*

When you cross paths with another,

dare to *make them smile.*

When you feel great,

dare to *help someone else feel great too.*

When the day has ended,

dare to feel as *you've done your best.*

Dare to be the best you can –

At all times, *Dare to be*!

- Steve Maraboli

Love creates a communion with life.
Love expands us, connects us,
sweetens us, ennobles us.
Love springs up in tender concern,
it blossoms into caring action.

It makes *beauty* out of all we touch.

In any moment we can step beyond our small self and

embrace each other as beloved parts of a whole.

- Jack Kornfield

These are the few ways we can practice
humility:

To speak as little as possible of one's self.
To mind one's own business.
Not to want to manage other people's affairs.
To avoid curiosity.
To accept contradictions and correction cheerfully.
To pass over the mistakes of others.
To accept insults and injuries.
To accept being slighted, forgotten and disliked.
To be kind and gentle even under provocation.
Never to stand on one's dignity.
To choose always the hardest.

- Mother Teresa

Don't just seek *happiness* when you're down.
Happiness shouldn't be a goal,
it should be a *habit*.
Take the focus off doing,
and start being every day.
Be *loving*, be *grateful*, be *helpful*,
and be a *spectator to your own thoughts*.

- Richard Branson

Develop an attitude of *gratitude,*
and give thanks for everything that
happens to you,
knowing that every step forward
is a step toward achieving
something bigger and
better than your current situation.

- Brian Tracy

Once you stand in your own *authenticity,*

you release the flow of sensuality that

frees you to be who you were meant to be.

- Lebo Grand

Life is a series of *natural* and *spontaneous changes.*
Don't resist them – that only creates sorrow.

Let reality be reality.

Let things *flow* naturally forward in

whatever way they like. - Lao Tzu

Hope and *purpose* in this world is

living as best as you can and

maybe having life that gives back.

But simply giving back isn't purpose;

it's a branch of purpose,

but it is not the trunk or

root of the tree.

- Nick Vujicic

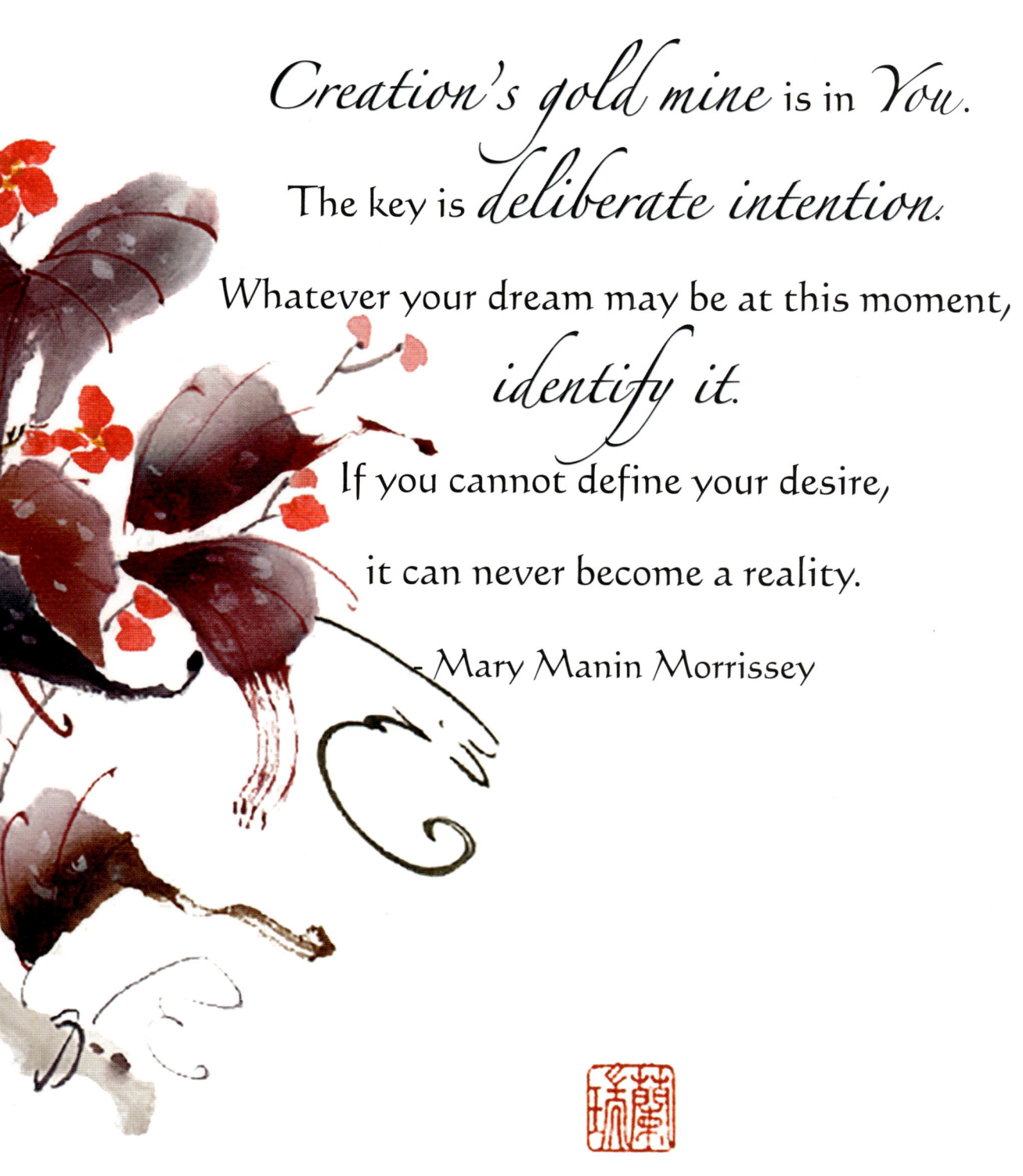

Creation's gold mine is in *You.*

The key is *deliberate intention.*

Whatever your dream may be at this moment,

identify it.

If you cannot define your desire,

it can never become a reality.

- Mary Manin Morrissey

Everyone has inside of him a piece of

good news.

The good news is that you

don't know how *great* you can be!

How much you can *love*!

What you can *accomplish*!

And what your *potential* is!

- Anne Frank

Love yourself...
enough to take the actions
required for your *happiness...*
enough to cut yourself loose
from the drama-filled past...
enough to set a *high standard*
for relationships...

enough to feed your mind and body
in a *healthy* manner...
enough to *forgive* yourself...
enough to *move on.*

- Steve Maraboli

Each *day* holds a *surprise.*
But only if we *expect it* can we see, hear,
or feel it when it comes to us.
Let's not be afraid to *receive* each day's surprise,
whether it comes to us as sorrow or as joy.
It will open a new place in our hearts,
a place where we can welcome new friends
and *celebrate* more fully our shared humanity.

- Henri Nouwen

I slept and dreamt
life is *beauty,*

I woke and found

life is *duty.*

- Confucius

Promise Yourself

To be so strong that
nothing can disturb
your peace of mind.
To talk health, happiness,
and prosperity to every person
you meet.
To make all your friends feel
that there is
something in them
To look at the sunny side
of everything and make
your optimism come true.
To think only the best, to work
only for the best,
and to expect only the best.
To be just as enthusiastic
about the success of others
as you are about your own.

To forget the mistakes of the past
and press on to the greater
achievements of the future.
To wear a cheerful countenance at all times
and give every living creature
you meet a smile.
To give so much time to the improvement of
yourself that you have no
time to criticize others.
To be too large for
worry, too noble for anger,
too strong for fear, and too happy to
permit the presence of trouble.
To think well of yourself and to proclaim
this fact to the world, not in loud words
but great deeds.
To live in faith that the whole world is
on your side so long as you are true to
the best that is in you.

- Christian D. Larson

I send you love!

About the Author

Photo courtesy of **CURTIS**VISION

Nan Rae, author of "What If...", is an artist, lecturer, social media influencer living in Southern California.

Her Brush Painting classes and book "The Ch'i of the Brush" have inspired thousands.

Heartfelt thanks to Curtis McElhinney, award winning photographer and videographer for this photo. curtisvision.com

 @nanraefineart

 NanRaeFineArt

nanraestudio.com

Mood Seals on the Cover

In Brush painting in addition to the personal name seal of the artist, mood or side seals are often used to enhance the painting.

 "Life Spent Like This Would Be Joyful Indeed"

 My personal name chop - "Auspicious Orchid"

 Back Cover:
"Floating Petals in the Stream and Thoughts of Meditation Together Compose One Harmony"